Where Do All the Puddles Go?

Contents

David Tunkin

RIGBY

Puddles

What happens when it rains?

When it rains, drops of water form puddles on the ground.

Have you ever wanted to know what happens to the water in a puddle?

Sunlight

What happens when it stops raining?

When it stops raining and the sun comes out,
the puddles start to dry up.
The sun shines onto the puddles. Sunlight
is warm, so it heats the water in the puddles.

Water vapour

What happens when water gets warm?

Heat from the sun can make water evaporate. When water **evaporates**, it turns into water vapour. We cannot see **water vapour**, but it is in the air.

Condensation

What happens when water rises?

Water vapour in the air cools down as it rises. As it cools down, the water vapour in the air turns back into tiny drops of water. This is called **condensation**.

Clouds

What happens to water drops?

As the water drops get bigger, they group together and form a cloud.

Water drops form a cloud

Wind blows the cloud across the sky

Water drops rise and get bigger

puddle

The clouds are blown across the sky by the wind. More water vapour joins the clouds from other puddles, and from rivers and the sea.

Water drops join the cloud from rivers and the sea

river

sea

Rain clouds

What happens to clouds?

As more water vapour joins a cloud, the drops in the cloud get bigger. Then the cloud gets bigger and darker and becomes a rain cloud.

Rain

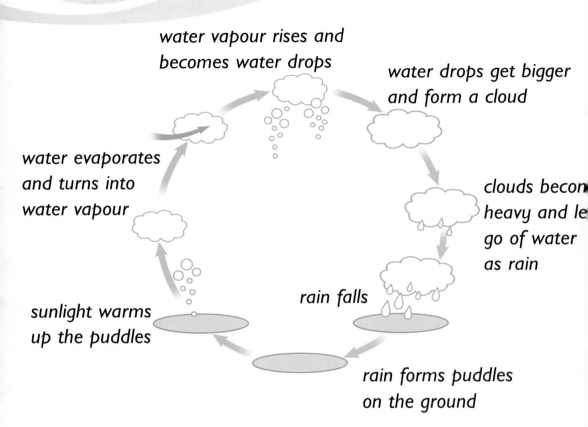

water vapour rises and becomes water drops

water drops get bigger and form a cloud

water evaporates and turns into water vapour

clouds becom[e] heavy and le[t] go of water as rain

sunlight warms up the puddles

rain falls

rain forms puddles on the ground

Why do clouds make rain?

When a rain cloud becomes too heavy, it lets go of some of its water. This falls as rain onto the ground. The rain forms more puddles, and so the **water cycle** begins again.

Glossary

condensation when water vapour cools down and forms drops of water

evaporates when water drops change into water vapour

water cycle when water turns into clouds and back to water again

water vapour when water evaporates it becomes vapour

Index